THE PASSENGER

THE PASSENGER
RICHARD FROUDE

SKYLIGHT PRESS

First published in Great Britain in 2012 by Skylight Press,
210 Brooklyn Road, Cheltenham, Glos GL51 8EA

Designed and typeset by Rebsie Fairholm
Publisher: Daniel Staniforth

Cover image: "Hide Under the Shadow of Your Wings" by Kathryn Mayo Winter and Doug Winter, used with permission of the artists. For more details see www.numberfivestudio.com

Text typeface is Monarcha by Isac Rodrigues, display fonts are Cioran and Ornamentus by Fernando Forero.

Printed and bound in Great Britain by Lightning Source, Milton Keynes

www.skylightpress.co.uk

ISBN 978-1-908011-38-1

As ever, for Rohini

CONTENTS

The Margaret Thatcher Trilogy

    Practical Maths (Exam Conditions)   11

    The Birds   19

    The Spectacle of Empire   27

    Practical Maths (TV Edit)   35

The History of Zero

    The Passenger   45

    The Surgeon's Daughter   77

    Songs for Birds and Rivers   91

THE
MARGARET THATCHER
TRILOGY

PRACTICAL MATHS (EXAM CONDITIONS)

Question One

A train leaves Lime Street at 10am heading south on the West Coast line.
Another leaves St Ives at one. Henry 8th sits at the window.
Both are travelling at 65 miles per hour. Both are only half full.
If all these things remain constant, how many wives did he have?
Six. And he engineered the break with Catholicism.
No, I'm thinking of a different train. I'm thinking of Steve.
Sorry no. The engineer is called Steve.
The train was once, twice, three times a lady.
Her names were Beatrice, Margaret and Jane. Margaret was the feisty one.
Ended up becoming Prime Minister and turning the others to stone.
Or was it gold? No. That's something else entirely.

Question Two

Let's try again.

A train leaves St Ives on Friday with an engineer named Steve.

I leave my house on foot with a cough.

Margaret Thatcher falls asleep on stage at the Conservative Party conference.

What is her average speed?

88. We don't have enough road to get to 88.

But we're travelling on rails.

Margaret Thatcher was the 66th wife of Henry the 88th.

The number is important to her.

Question Three

An engineer leaves a train at 72 miles per hour.
It is raining in St Ives.
Henry 8th seems glum today. He is lonely and talking to statues.
Beatrice looks at him through stone eyes. She says nothing.
Steve locates the Conservative Club off Lime Street.
Jane has escaped from Catholicism and is running through a cemetery.
Her stone legs drag.
Margaret and I are napping together.

Question Four

Beatrice discovers trigonometry. She follows a tangent to Lime Street.
We meet heading south on the West Coast line.
Jane wanders into the Conservative Club at 3 miles per hour.
Steve is at the bar, talking shop. Coffee and sugar drinks are cyanide to
  machines.
Henry 8th boards a train in St Ives at 3pm.
We pass him at 43 degrees.
Jane joins Steve at the bar.
Margaret is standing on the platform at Crewe.
The exact moment when the two trains meet.

Question Five

Jane leaves Steve at 11pm. She has whiskey on her breath.
Henry 8th has a job cleaning windows at the Conservative Club.
I am falling in love with Beatrice at a speed of 12 miles per hour.
She has caught my cough.
Margaret is researching angles.
In St Ives a man realizes that he has more wives than Henry 8th.
The West Coast line is lilting. It has become obtuse.

Question Six

Steve dreams about becoming a statue.
Beatrice and I are in St Ives, staying with a sculptor.
She sits up in bed and mentions tuberculosis.
She talks of her sisters.
Henry 8th looks through windows and begins to understand.
He is not lonely any more.
I worry about Margaret. She is sullen these days.
Jane sits in the smoking car but dreams about the buffet.
The Conservative Club is empty.

Question Seven

Jane leaves her body at 6am and hovers above the West Coast line.
It remains in stone on the platform at Lime Street.
Margaret is staring and trying to remember.
She was going to St Ives with her sisters.
She met a man and something changed.
She became Prime Minister and married the King. But something
  changed her sisters.
Steve has discovered Medusa in library books.
Henry 8th has settled in a bungalow by the sea.
Beatrice gives me stone kisses in the parlour.
She is dying at a speed of 12 miles per hour.
If all these things remain constant, what colour are her eyes?
I don't know.
Let me repeat the question. What colour are her eyes?
Brown. Maybe brown.

THE BIRDS

Phase One: Infrastructure

Archaeopteryx was the first bird.
He would glide over flightless sauropods.
Beat his wings from rocky promontories.
A new evolution of feathered pride.
But lonely he stood, under green cretaceous skies.

Phase Two: Mobilization

I am reading stories of an aging parrot.
A vocabulary of 900 words, the ability to phrase them.
This is more advanced than chimps.
And they made movies about chimps.
The parrot is approaching 80. He grows increasingly sarcastic.
A dry, sometimes cruel sense of humour.

I endure conversations with penguins.
I stand in their Gardens, unkempt and pressed to the glass.
The children have a name for me.
I am pursuing intelligence.
We are losing the war.

Phase Three: Subversion

7 years old: my family is given two pheasants by the local farmer.
A billiards acquaintance of my father but we are never country folk.
The pheasants hang by their feet in the garage.
My grandmother's round to pluck them.
The sink is full of entrails and blood drips onto linoleum.
In the dining room, my father remarks that this is the smell of death.
We order pizza.

Phase Four: Camouflage

Penguins wear dinner suits.
This is what people say.
We give them names like King or Emperor, but they never answer.
I am imagining an empire without language.
Most of the children are orphans.
They stand beside me, pressed to the glass.

I am reading Thomas Wolfe.
I am reading a short paragraph that charts the evolution of life on this
  planet.
Look Homeward Angel, he has forgotten the birds.

Winston Churchill kept a parrot.
He also kept a dog. He called his sadness a black dog.
I am Archaeopteryx, misunderstanding Churchill's parrot.
He is squawking about the Nazis.
I want him to fly with me, over to the Gardens.
We shall fight them on the beaches.

Phase Five: Strategic Intelligence

Margaret Thatcher has grown into mythology, her skin wrought of iron.
Wings have sprouted, organic and batlike.
She has no need for feathers.
She has no need for old eyes. She deals instead in sound.

Once upon a time she both was and was not.
Once upon a time, empirically speaking, she simultaneously both was
and was not.
Once upon this isolated moment, she grew in a fashion that could not be
considered linear.
Once among the non-linear, questions were asked of breadth and depth.
She both answered and did not answer.
She both spoke and remained silent.
She both expanded in a fashion that could not be considered linear and
contracted, quite gradually, until she could not be seen.

She is growing her fingernails.
We shall cut into her stomach and find, perhaps, the Falklands.
Arthur Scargill, and a lobe of Reagan's ear.
She is naked of blue dresses.
No longer bears a torch but has lit her fist aflame.

Phase Six: Engagement

They have drawn ranks now, the penguins and the orphans.
Thomas Wolfe sides with the children.
Thatcher leads the birds.
Winston Churchill has dissolved into the talons of his parrot.
A dog barks in the Gardens.

Oscar Wilde knew nightingales.
A volley from the pheasants. The orphans stand their ground.
Penguins group beside me, pressed to the glass.
Wolfe remains undaunted.

Oscar Wilde knew nightingales.
He understood the blood that dripped onto linoleum.
I am reading Winston Churchill.
We give him names like King or Emperor.

I am wearing a dinner suit tight over feathers.
I could have been flightless.
Sick with evolution.

Phase Seven: Permanent Echo

Churchill swoops down to rest on my shoulder.
Thatcher regurgitates a sink full of entrails.
The orphans have devoured all 900 words.

Archaeopteryx descends, a non-linear wingspan.
The Falklands arise from Thatcher's split colon.
Wolfe runs rampant. He shatters the glass.

The penguins march on Westminster.
It contracts, quite gradually, until it cannot be seen.
Thatcher is screeching through the spires.
Orphans lie depleted in the Gardens.
Churchill, the parrot, draws blood from my shoulder and whispers:
We are more advanced than chimps.
We are more advanced than chimps, my friend.
We are more advanced than chimps but we are losing the war.

THE SPECTACLE OF EMPIRE

First Movement

When I was younger, I had dreams about Margaret Thatcher.
I had dreams about running through cobblestone streets.
Now I dream about Richard Nixon.
He wears woollen overcoats and hobnail boots.
I try to find context for these dreams.
I swing with clenched fists but never connect.

These were younger – of course – much younger, more vulnerable years.
When refrigerators were skyscrapers.
When I stared up to blue kitchen cabinets and tarried over cobblestones
  at the weir.

    This is Richard Nixon.
    These dreams are inappropriate.
    This is an inappropriate city.

These are – of course – more vulnerable years.
And I am older now. Old enough that we can marry.
I can buy you liquor, take you home and we can fuck.

    There is no Nixon.
    These are my clenched fists.
    This is us, fucking.

And I appreciate the streets of this city.
I appreciate our walks in the shade of refrigerators.
I can't stand the sun, sometimes.
I can't stand to see us married inside blue kitchen cabinets.
I have purchased a fire extinguisher and ...

There is no Nixon.
There are no cobblestone streets.
It is beautiful, right now, to be inappropriate.
Here is my fire extinguisher.

These are our walks through more vulnerable years when we could not
understand disgust.
When we marvelled at the sun and left everything to the imagination.

Second Movement

I have tried to reconcile various dreams.
On cobblestones, I lie and find this city in the rivets.
I wield this fire extinguisher as if it were a weapon.
I can buy you liquor, if you want. We can keep it in blue kitchen cabinets.
Catch our disgust in clenched fists.

    These are not cobblestones.
    This is Margaret Thatcher.
    This is me, fucking Margaret Thatcher.
    This is Margaret Thatcher sipping cheap liquor from a
      fire extinguisher.

I told you, I am older now.
I can buy you things with clenched fists.
I can buy you this city, this cobblestone sun.
We are most comfortable when inappropriate.
Most beautiful in disgust.
I used to confuse disgust with loneliness.
We were pitiful then.
I have tried to say sorry.

I cannot make this beautiful.
Cannot find shade or the means to afford it.
I continue to swing but cannot connect.
There is something quite sinister here.
What is it you expect we will find?

This is a city built entirely of ...
This is me staring back.
This is our private means of escape.

These are the ways I attempt to find refuge.
I dismantle my body and rebuild it with light.
I forget my own features. Fail to recognize my eyes.
I drift between inappropriate presentations of myself.
Persuade myself I'll find myself in the city's filthy rivets.
I am older now and penniless.
I can't buy you this disgust.
It would be nice to settle down perhaps, buy you things with light.

We tell each other to be open.
That we don't know what we'll run from.
It is useless to look back now, find the language of this city.

I am sinking into Nixon.
I have turned the fire extinguisher on myself.
Doused my clothes with liquor but failed to find a spark.

Third Movement

Lately I have felt like an Angel.
I drift about balconies of the highest skyscrapers, unable to afford
　anything but language.
I fail to recognize myself.
I continue to purchase.
I joke about disgust and pretend I could take you home.
This was when we could look at each other.
When liquor and language and fucking were enough.

I had a job inside a skyscraper.
This is me, as Richard Nixon, with a job inside a skyscraper.

It was nice to have something that placed me inside.
Nice not to drift. Without wings or language.
They told me it was.
I found it hard to believe. Easy to touch.
And it is hard for me to touch you now.
I have lost the door to the skyscraper.
I need back in.
I am disguised as Richard Nixon but the doorman is suspicious.

　　This is me, disguised as Richard Nixon, unable to touch you and
　　with no money for liquor.

　　And this is the job I always wanted.
　　And this is the job I got when I abandoned language and seduced
　　　Margaret Thatcher in the shade of another refrigerator.
　　And this is the job I have now: to scale an abandoned skyscraper,
　　　clothe myself in language, raise money to purchase new fire
　　　extinguishers, new liquor and a fresh sense of touch.

And I will turn this skyscraper into a museum.
I will exhibit various portions of this life in the shade.
Old wings, a liquor bottle, cobblestones, my disgust.
You, your language, my clenched fists, my am.
The idea has become ludicrous.

There is no elevator to take me.
I can see you, waving from penthouse windows.
There are too many things I am able to touch.
And all I have are these things.

I tack images of us to skyscraper windows.
We are naked and laughing.
We are gathering language and letting it go.
There is no one to touch us.
No disgust to run from.

These are – of course – more vulnerable years.
This is – of course – no time other than now.
I have found no means of escape except cobblestones, this anger.
I separate objects of life in the shade.

PRACTICAL MATHS
(TV EDIT)

Scene One

An analogue clock. 10am in the gymnasium. You may begin writing now.
Portly man occupies leather seat inside a glass museum case.
Fade over Ordnance Survey map of the British Isles.
In the gymnasium an invigilator paces down rows of desks.
Clichéd executioner, hooded, swinging an axe.
A seismograph begins slight undulations.
Then levels off.
Three-carriage diesel locomotive pulls away.
Library footage: Thatcher speaking in the Commons.
Library footage: Thatcher holding up three fingers outside 10 Downing Street, 1987.
An Assyrian image of Midas.

Scene Two

Return to analogue clock.
Return to map of British Isles.
A grey front door slams shut.
Library footage: Thatcher drifts off.
Gymnasium, the invigilator's pencil snaps.
An energy flash. The DeLorean appears and speeds across a now-existent
bridge.
Doc Brown's second time machine follows momentarily with sons Jules
and Verne.
Man in museum case, previous image multiplied into eleven columns
of eight.
Thatcher jerks awake.

Scene Three

Return to map of British Isles printed over with lines of binary code.

A weatherman winces.

A child appears in the museum case, above and in front of the seated man.

Girl at café table, reading, we cannot see her face.

A shudder on the seismograph.

A caterpillar begins to cocoon.

It is struggling.

Thatcher knocks on the grey front door.

Scene Four

Over café girl's shoulder, zoom to her page: Da Vinci's *Il Corpo Umano*.
Map now tacked to grey front door.
The cocoon continues to form. A high speed shot.
The seismograph has settled.
Glass case child begins to rotate. The portly man stares up.
Floor plan: Great Pyramid of Giza.
The cocoon rolls over a graphic page.
Ordnance Survey Detail: Crewe and Surrounding Area.
The invigilator sighs.

Scene Five

Cocoon rolls to the floor. The impact registers on the seismograph.
The child has passed through one revolution. A music box accompanies.
Opposite café girl. She looks up with brown eyes.
And hold this shot.
Thatcher is surprised by the tacked map.
The weatherman smiles.
And the map is blurring. The coast appears to be shifting.

Scene Six

Seismographic fluctuations as we have never seen.
Same café girl opens grey front door to the set of the Weather Report.
An expression of surprise.
She holds up three fingers, as Thatcher, '87.
Behind glass the man stands and reaches to his child. A small crowd
has gathered.
Their fingers touch.
Front Page Headline: Thatcher Resigns.
The cocoon rests on linoleum.
Effect of film reel igniting.

Scene Seven

The cocoon splits. Butterfly clicks.
Zoom to abandoned shell, backdrop of perfect dock leaf.
Closer still, we can see the veins.
The Weather's on all three channels.
Music box reprise.
Carriages detach from the diesel engine.
The seismograph pulses in uniform rhythm.
Glass case now empty of man and child. The leather seat remains.
Flash to the café, repetition of girl looking up.
Her eyes are now closed.
The invigilator checks his watch.
No more parachutes.
The invigilator checks his watch.
Would you stop writing please.

THE
HISTORY OF
ZERO

THE PASSENGER

I

Confession:

I've never grown out of aeroplane windows. I mean, in the way I've grown out of the Dinosaur Club. Nor have I grown out of my body underwater. I will always need this appropriation of weightlessness as I will always need this expression of distance:

II

Complication:

Vinelike, I have grown out of aeroplane windows. Over Kentucky, then Xante and her pregnant neighbour. The Canadian plains, Colorado and Montana. But in Kentucky, I made acquaintance with Design. And I sat in the window seat, and upon recently varnished decks, and swam in their swimming pools, and tried to reclaim Kentucky for Zero.

III

Design, an imposition, born from the perfunctory intercourse of Commerce and the American Church. Commerce, like the Pope, refusing contraception.

So gestation began in the bowels of the Church. And Americans came, and they purchased, and Zero wept in the stockrooms. And Design, I have learnt, was born in Irvine, California.

IV

Where there is nothing, we must put something.
Where there are deserts, we will redirect rivers and build polythene cities.
Where there is fertility, we will impregnate.
And Americans will come, and they will purchase, and Zero will weep in
the vestry.

I am not writing about the fall of man.

But a biography of Design, who is the darkness of set loam, who in
dreams rolls through quiet streets on life support, paisley pyjamas, a
grin on his grey face.

But a memoir of Zero, whose name is Celandine, dining on scraps
beneath the communion table. Head in her hands. Then laughing,
underwater, from this inexplicable distance, weightless and improving,
sad eyed concubine of Loss. Action's original lover. On a postcard of
Tripoli. A face in the patchwork. Everybody's aunts sewn together in a
coarse blanket. Awakens on fire in an empty room. Awakens submerged
in America. Sleeps in public restrooms outside of Denver on I-70. Passes
through customs with the desert in her pocket. Redirected, so that Las
Vegas has clean water. A lark. An albatross. Three coins, retrieved from
the Trevy fountain. There is too much water here.

V

Where there is nothing, we must put something.
From aeroplane windows, there are swimming pools. Curves.
Where we live must have a symmetrical partner.
So there will be someone waiting just for us.
Here, symmetry to counteract solitude.

VI

Design is a man, but like all men has a mother. Zero is a woman, but like all women has suffered for Design. Zero is a Canadian wilderness. My limbs are cirrus clouds. I am not writing about the fall of man but a history of mirrors and loam.

Celandine is a swallow. A swallow is a bird. A bird must breathe. Celandine is her breath. Swimming pools attract mosquitoes at night. And swimming pools, I have learnt, were born in Irvine, California. It was a swallow, not a dove, who carried an olive branch to the Philistines.

There are doctors in the desert. They are replacing my skin with crêpe paper, my heart with a transistor. The sand is packed tight and I am growing inside it.

I will weep with Montana upon the blankets of orphans. Whose fathers left their mothers and whose mothers left the tenements. My skin will be sewn into shades for their windows. Behind their windows I will sit above Kentucky. Design will make jokes at my symmetrical expense.

VII

Design creeping through Xante with tourism on his breath. Impregnating the space between islands. Crawling originally from the oceans to alight in the desert. He redirects the valves of internal mechanics to sprout cities on the plains. By cities, I mean hospitals built of sand. Or tenements whose purpose is incubation. He recruits orphans with promises of blankets and distance.

VIII

Design holed up in public restrooms outside of Denver on I-70. Finding a simple altar there and burning the restrooms to the ground. And from the ashes, incorporating new suburbs. Consecrating swimming pools. Grounding the last aeroplanes.

IX

Where will I go without this distance?
Zero, I hear you coughing in the night.

I will send you postcards from Tripoli, as Tripoli, I have learnt, is a
suburb of Irvine, California. Meet me in Montana where we can grow
out of our bodies and alight as manna from Heaven. Are there lowlands
in Montana? What limbs will we carry?

X

The secret lives of mirrors, weightlessness and loam.

XI

There is too much water here. I am driving to Montana in a flatbed pickup. There are stories I haven't told you. And I must tell you these stories because you understand. What it is to be between continents. The refractions of aeroplane windows. This, our personal history of Zero:

Design illustrates thousands of ways that two improbably attractive people can find each other. These are stories about symmetry. I must tell you about a house built entirely of driftwood, reclaimed from the ocean like the lowlands themselves. Our tremendous sensitivity to earthquakes. The rituals we employ to carry our dead.

XII

At every rest stop I investigate the soil:

1. A fellowship derived from the mutual desire to evaluate acidity. So we found each other through acidity, and acidity was our sustenance. A dinner conversation. A joke shared only with eyes. In the event of a drop in cabin pressure, oxygen masks will deploy from the ceiling in front of you. Your seat cushion can be used as a flotation device. I take samples until I am completely satisfied. Then move on.

2. Am I losing you? If it looks like a human and it smells like a human, then by Design, it must be a human. This apparatus detects traces of crêpe paper in the soil. Occasionally, I bake, substituting silicon for sugar. This reminds me, wanting for a scrap of paper. A keepsake. What did you write upon windows as a child?

3. The Nile is the longest river in the world. The Amazon is the longest river in the world. The Severn is the longest river in the world. The Danube is the longest river in the world. Dresden was known as the Florence of the Elbe. Leipzig was known as the Florence of the Elbe. Count to twenty then open your eyes. Coming, ready or not.

4. My father grew up on the English side of the Severn. My mother on the Welsh side. John Betjeman described Clifton as the most beautiful suburb in Europe. Dylan Thomas described Swansea as the graveyard of ambition. I never really cared for John Betjeman. I'll ask you again, am I losing you? These are all issues of acidity.

Try these experiments at home.

XIII

Digital Zero is a crisp silence though I droop consistently towards the analogue. Montana is a house built entirely of driftwood. Design is itself a mirror. A grate set into the floor. Any tea or coffee, sir? Any tea or coffee at all? Hot snack? The captain has turned on the fasten seatbelt sign. I don't know how much longer I can do this without you.

XIV

Beretta drove her car to the Severn. Beretta whose name is Celandine. Whose nature is Zero. Beretta who is the longest river in the world.

Her car was not a flatbed and the Severn is not in Montana. Nor is it outside of Denver or anywhere on I-70. Although everything, except Denver, is by Design outside of Denver.

I should understand this by now. As I should understand Commerce and gymnasiums. As I have learnt to understand baseball. Just yesterday I said handbrake when I meant parking brake and for a moment everything was ruined. Much of my dialect is gathered from original Kentucky conversation. This film has been altered from its original format, it has been modified to fit this screen.

XV

Where there are deserts, we will redirect rivers and build polythene
cities. Beretta finds herself in Las Vegas, a community of doctors. The
shortest distance between two people is a smile. A smile is all teeth.
And smiles, I have learnt, were born in Irvine, California. Many of these
procedures may appear cosmetic. At every rest stop I bathe in the soil.

XVI

Design is a doctor. Zero is Montana. Commerce is the most beautiful suburb in Europe. Irvine, California is a hospital on the banks of the longest river in the world. John Betjeman is himself a mirror. A transistor is more reliable than a traditional human heart. My limbs are cirrus clouds. Celandine is the tenement. I am the machine.

XVII

Q: If all of this is true, then I am a passenger on an aeroplane somewhere above Kentucky. Where am I going?

A: Montana. No. If I am on this aeroplane I am not going to Montana because I am going to Montana in a flatbed pickup.

All of this is true.

Q: Is all of this true only by Design?

A: If I wake up in Montana then this is not true. I didn't realize I was sleeping. There is no such thing as fiction.

It occurs that perhaps I am Montana. That my growth, vinelike, is something mechanical not animal. My head is in Billings but my heart is in Missoula. Outside Ottawa, I kept regular appointments with an albino Iranian barber named Khalil. Ottawa is not in Montana. Nor is it in Xante. His shop was located in the Billings Bridge complex. If nothing else, this is true.

I am Montana behind windows looking out over Kentucky in an unknown conveyance. Much depends on whether I am airborne. But everything has always been airborne.

XVIII

Q: Is this a story? Or a dictionary? What is an intransitive poetic?

A: When Beretta drove her car to the Severn she built a bridge to Zero.

Q: Or was the bridge Zero? Or was it Celandine who drove her car to the Severn?

A: There are two bridges that connect England and Wales. I am neither of these bridges. I am an aeroplane. I am frequently dizzy and my name is Zero. Design is itself a mirror. A grate set into the floor.

XIX

Q: Is an arc by its nature complete? In such case, is its nature Design?
Can this nature make wit of contradictions? I'm not sure if I have
anything to give you.

A: In my most frequent dream, I find you sleeping in the lilacs. You sit
up and look to the window. There is something terrible outside but we
are safe here. You tell me this quietly. The words form images before me,
and they shimmer with perfect diction.

On the seventh day I open the grate. Inside is a miniature coffin. Inside
the coffin is a pinwheel of red oak leaves but the red is too deliberate.
The grate is set in the floor of a public restroom outside of Denver on
I-70. This will be our definition of weightlessness.

I blow on the pinwheel. The leaves turn and blow back onto my face.
They reveal memories, afternoons before Kristallnacht. One day, they
say, we will live together beneath the grate and beget new images of love
among the lilacs. They will paint their stories onto your body, and I will
be the winds across Montana.

Celandine, I hear you coughing in the night.
I write you letters on peacock feathers, plucked from the tails of dying
  friends.
Unable to send them I make pinwheels and bury them in miniature
  coffins.
Where there is nothing, we must put something.

XX

Q: Am I teasing you?

A: A parade of confessions:

1. I have begun to think of this as a painting. Matisse says he paints the things he wants to see. By Matisse, I mean Picasso. By Picasso I mean that I do not know what this would look like if I could see it. This will be our definition of loam.

2. I am uncertain whether the things I have stated with such conviction are true. In fact, I have no recollection of writing many of those things. This will be our definition of a river.

3. I have developed an acute sensitivity to earthquakes. I am aware of even the slightest tremor. This may be related to my intimacy with the soil. By the soil, I mean Celandine. By Celandine, I mean the moment when seismology takes a lover.

4. I have begun to think of this as a series of fluctuations.

5. The shortest distance between two people is not a smile. It is Zero. The shortest distance between symmetry and loss is Design. The shortest distance between Design and Zero is a mirror.

With all this in mind, we may have a new geography.

Q: What is the longest river in the world?

XXI

Beretta lay down outside the hospital. And I watched as the orphans stamped on her gentle arms.

XXII

The Doctors evolved from a Kentucky tribe originally confined to the periphery. Their cooperation with Design enabled movement toward the interior through a network of gymnasiums. Here, the gymnasium functions much like the early Church: a place of fellowship, a physical centre where members find support. New gymnasiums are consecrated with the names of elders, posthumous converts, or simply the city that the gymnasium replaces. Always in perfect symmetry, they may be constructed in minutes. Although most are built of set loam, there are several instances of sand, mirrors, or water as a substitute.

XXIII

Here, fossilization as the gradual intercourse of death and loam.
Beretta as my body underwater.

XXIV

In Xante, Doctors discover remains of a new species of dinosaur. Their conclusions are published orally:

Cruciform patterns throughout the bone structure. Mirrored scales across the breastplate, presumably a defence mechanism. Perhaps feathered with plumage similar to the modern day peacock. Able to subsist on soil but with a preference for lilacs. Likely to have roamed West, as far as Irvine, California.

Here, existence as repetition.

XXV

The result is something like a street map but the cities are replaced with colour. Matisse says he thinks of his paintings as such maps. By Matisse, I mean Matisse. By paintings, I mean that if I can shoot rabbits, then I can shoot fascists. But I have never shot a rabbit, a fascist, a lark or an albatross.

XXVI

In the event of an emergency landing over water, your skin can be used as a flotation device. Design maintains that fiction is possible, if one can determine the appropriate gradient of descent. Hydrogen is a signature for water. Water is a signature for life. And life, here, is underwritten by Design.

XXVII

Q: Peacock, lark, albatross.

A: Hospital, city, gymnasium.

Q: Raccoon, samba, waltz.

A: Hat, scarf, ear.

XXVIII

In my left arm I keep a fear of dogs. A fear of bees in my right. The soil informs me of a world without the distinctions of language. Let's talk about this on the telephone. The use of electronic devices is permitted only when the cabin doors are open. In review, a way to open the doors.

The memory of a river: a meadow to one side. Dogs splash in the shallows. The orphans toss them food but the dogs will not touch it. By food, I mean their dead. Only one, the largest, tears flesh from a canine skeleton. The orphans whoop. The cannibal dog has the head of a man.

I tell Beretta this story. She asks about the bees. When I was seven I trod on a wasp. Here, flight as the contrary of death. A wasp is not a bee. How do you know? You weren't there. In review, a way to reinforce solitude.

The cannibal dog has the head of a man. These are developments beyond Design, as Beretta would portray herself. An anomaly, with plumage similar to the modern day peacock. Able to subsist on soil but with a preference for lilacs.

I have taken to sleeping in a miniature coffin. Everything I know I learned from birds.

XXIX

She cannot believe in dinosaurs because she is still amazed by the size of sea birds. All of this, despite our childhoods on the causeway. My poor, cold Beretta. This, perhaps, an incidental elegy.

To be a passenger, one requires a conveyance and a driver. I remember, under coarse blankets, we were headed to the border. Montana, now, as a new brand of heaven.

XXX

I have never grown out of you, Celandine. I mean, in the way I am
growing out of these miniature coffins. I have followed you through
aeroplane windows. To the spaces occupied by Zero. A house built
entirely of driftwood, a grate set into the floor.

Illuminated by Commerce, these rituals we employ to carry our dead. A
tightness in the shoulders treated with loam and symmetry.

Any tea or coffee, sir?
Over Kentucky, your reflection as Zero.
Any tea or coffee at all?

Beretta, I hear you coughing in the night.
Your body, retrieved from the Trevy fountain.
A lark. An albatross.
These were his notes from the continent.

THE SURGEON'S DAUGHTER

XXXI

Raised in a blue land, though paler lines ran through it. My poor, cold
Beretta. Skin hung on a glass skeleton. How a name can itself be named.

Design finds virtue in its inevitability. Every breath a prototype, so that
respiration becomes a creative act. Fear of flying. Fear of birds. These are
not regrets, rather, interludes I have lived over and over.

XXXII

High tides submerge the causeway. We steal food from fishermen, sleep
under sackcloth in the lifeboat house. She feels something pulling at
her. We are both familiar with gravity, his ability to escape blame. She
wants to think of her life as a series of fluctuations. We try pacing our
heartbeats with a seismograph.

Although there is nothing specific I can bring her, I am aware of a lack.
She says this proves we are alive. There are procedures to atone for this,
although many appear cosmetic.

XXXIII

She is mostly blank but Mays about her centre in russet and gold.
These are colours with histories. Colours of homecoming and October
is homecoming in the sense that she can still find a gallon of milk for
under a dollar. Of course it isn't milk at all. This is the influence of gold,
our dyslexic alchemy. Of course it isn't a gallon because a gallon requires
number and there is no number in October, only in its name.

We spend these days on straight roads and ignore the soil. We learn
songs about the sun and recite them at rest stops. Some of our songs
are only one or two syllables. In this way, we begin to differentiate
between stops. So develops our geography as an assignment of music.
Here, realism as the future of abstraction, the first notes of our nascent
language.

XXXIV

The last Muslims are executed in Xante. Gone now are the Quakers, the Shakers, the Mormons, the Moonies, the Christians, the Jews, the Sikhs, the Scientologists, the Hindus, the Wiccans, the Buddhists, the Pagans, the Zoroastrians, the Satanists, the Monarchists, the Eroticists, all other organised religions. There is only Design, intelligent and otherwise.

Attempts to synchronize our dreams. A visible network of wires across the sky. She stands at the window and will not turn away. We will plant lilacs here, in the desert. We must adapt to a world without moisture. Amphetamines, barbiturates, nitrogen and dust.

XXXV

Unity is truth. Beretta shits on this notion. She receives a telegram from her father. There are whispers of Zero in Kentucky, rumours of an underground city. I imagine the causeway but say nothing. Here, our two modes of immersion: water, loam.

Winter arrives as an awareness of our bodies. Now growing opaque, we must share our skin to keep warm. I calculate true north by the shade of her limbs. It is inevitable that Design will find the orphans.

The solstice passes quietly. Although many expire around us, their names remain.

XXXVI

How our lives ride upon a dreamt world. We are passengers, Beretta. To be weightless is to exert a force of Zero on this world.

Popular cartography records a river some miles east of Irvine, California. We will observe from this distance. Remember the causeway on cool linen.

Flight as a dream. Then flight as the actuality of our existence. There are certain techniques to achieve invisibility, particular songs, houses built entirely of driftwood.

If the Severn bursts its banks, it will flood the lowlands. We prepared for this as children. And we are still children, digging shelter into the earth, singing songs to Celandine.

XXXVII

The rare talent of her thought: to synthesize a tactile experience. Nine days since the telephone rang. Eight since she threw it out the window. We settle on a new covenant: my blood, siphoned into a common reservoir, The Nile as mere tributary.

She has lived these lives over and over in dreams. Her joints will systematically erode until —
Our meals taken in hospital canteens, I can only begin from premises of love and death. Mobility. Deconstruction. Both are possible outcomes of our century.

XXXVIII

What began in her as sympathy now manifests as violence. I want to change with her so I cut into my arm. Her father insists upon form, he arranges an efficiency near the hospital. If she is to be healed, we must find a doctor willing to assume her disease.

The equinox is meaningless. Deconstruction looms as a ritual to produce dust, worthless when new varieties of loam remain possible. I petition for alternative prognoses. Her skin a hallowed raiment.

Despite my fear of disease, I marry the surgeon's daughter.

XXXIX

I have collected several pamphlets on rebirth, the parental relation of question and answer. As a child, my father washed my hands with holy water. I stood at the sink and watched sea birds on the causeway.

The holy water arrived in a green bottle because green was the colour of heaven.

XL

Carriage to the mainland will take six days. To avoid Xante we must transfer in Tripoli. There are too many variables, she says. If departure is even possible, it is unlikely she will survive the voyage. This is unacceptable, she says. She refuses to die in transit.

Springtime is established as a mask. A new occlusive rhetoric. As long as her father is listening, she will not grant emotion to these discussions. So it remains. Unacceptable.

XLI

We bury April on D-Day. The ceremony is unorthodox as she was the
fourth and we are now the sixth. We spend the nines in the shade and
travel through the eights. It is cooler then.

Such is my desire to add to the record, entries stretch to include even the
most apparently trivial excursions. This is not without complication:
a journey requires not only a destination but a point of departure.
Unable to cement a singular origin, the list is developed to include both
destination and departure. No movement will escape the account.

Here, the destination becomes the origin.
Zero grows fluid.

XLII

A: The poem occurs in Zero but language exists only in Design. Good and evil are empty terms. I have taken to wearing a copper mask.

Q: It is easier to understand as an invisible membrane between worlds. As a child I collected dinosaurs, aeroplanes and ghosts. Does this make more sense?

A: When the war is over we can holiday in Tripoli. It begins as a private affair, death still a novelty. I attend merely as Beretta's guest.

Novelty gives way to number.
Silence where there should be punctuation.
In Zero there is no grail.
In Zero, only blood.

XLIII

Beretta insists upon driving. She has carved a map into her forearm. A world without the distinctions of language. The notation or gap left to indicate emptiness.

Despite my fear of disease, we bathe in the Severn. She grows weaker in the evenings. A swallow. The Elbe. I rarely feel the need to apologise. My occupancy here is a function of memory. On occasion a draft of remorse, a defunct currency valuable only to collectors.

Beretta lies down outside the hospital.
I watch as the orphans stamp on her gentle arms.

SONGS FOR BIRDS & RIVERS

XLIV

The Nile

In Zero there exists the Ideal, a wordless literature.

A pronounced symmetry between the divine and magical, in this instance: green. Of course, these are not the real bones but careful reproductions. It is not known whether the plates stood perpendicular to the spine or. Various tropes associated with the Trinity.

The living, the dead, the birth of the skin trade, rodents the size of small horses.

The proposition is Zero. Design as a garment. The greatest riddle is that we occupy bodies. So we experiment with various predicates: action, breath, existence.

The Ideal has no body.
Above all else, God must be weightless.

XLV

A Lark

We encounter a theory that the dinosaurs evolved into birds that in turn evolved into rivers. Similarly, the tower of Babel, continental drift, substance, and archangels. In caves beneath the Danube, an asemic manuscript to perplex Design.

Along the four arms of the city inhabitants may find all the requisite bolsters of a productive existence. The influence of Atlantis remains in concentric foundations. This is, of course, no accident. So runs the myth of Irvine, California.

XLVI

The Amazon

Gravity is not a predicate.
The Ideal does not speak.
I smell death on your hands.

Freedom is a city in California, a connection of strip malls.
There is no sand on Severn Beach.
The remaining population of Xante standing shoulder to shoulder.
Something for the little ones to stand on, please. I can't see their faces.

The Ideal is merely a name for Zero. My uncle invented the wheel.
God invented the wheel.
Zero invented God.

XLVII

An Albatross

Q: The argument for displacement.

A: The slow rise to prominence of one genus over another.

Q: Ceres, Pluto, Eris.

A: The minutes of this summit recorded and stored in caves beneath the Danube.

Q: The continuing accident of birth.

A: The interstice between two mirrors.

Q: This, the seat of activity.

A: Marsupials, primates, birds.

Q: This drawing is a photograph. This lithograph is a mosaic. This blueprint is a cipher.

A: The unwavering presence of the divine.

Q: There is something concentric happening in the desert.

A: A certain cadence that reminds her of her father.

Q: This is my beloved son, listen to him.

XLVIII

The Danube

Stegosaurus, Archaeopteryx, The Sphinx, Orion. All may be mythical if
necessary. Will you join the game, sir? The riddle does not exist.

Headsets are available for a small charge. Please close your eyes and
draw three coins from this polythene bag. The Greek drachma, the
Portuguese escudo, the Cypriot pound, the Austrian shilling, the Hong
Kong dollar. The habit of recording our history as a list. In adding a
song, a journey, the list grows as a phantom limb.

A cloud is not a phantom.
The passage from birth to death.
An aeroplane window.
Language as defunct currency.

Value is not a predicate. In its purest form, the poem escapes the
influence of gravity. As: if a ball is dropped time after time toward
infinity, it will eventually fall upwards.

Even when faced with extinction, evolution may appear as a novelty.
You are a turncoat, sir.
A sphinx in azure.
The sky over Billings.

XLIX

A Swallow

I believe in the eminence of sung language. I believe in the mutability of deities. I have grown submerged in America and carried the tropes of Design. I am mapping the coastline of your islands. I record your teachings on my limbs.

Literal meaning is a figment of Design. We meet only as symbols. No key is appropriate.

There are answers in the space between continents but it is clear that these answers are orphans. I will divine the questions that begat them. I will ignore the patterns of Watson and Pereira. So evolves a semantic surrogacy, not an exercise in truth but in substance. After all, Caesar would not be Caesar if he had not crossed the Severn. The Amazon. The Nile. The Rubicon.

L

The Elbe

What begins as an account of the interior must focus eventually on
the periphery. It is from the outsider that the nature of a society may
be gleaned. Their language, the manner of their exile. Honesty follows
a fluidity of the conceptual home, a perpetual flight, though this is
neither exclusive nor failsafe.

You may notice the absence of biographical detail. In its place, various
ablatives of an obscure declension. Formulaic? Perhaps. But this is the
nature of Design. To destroy one must first become, as is their custom of
healing. These rituals should be observed before appropriation.

With what authority do I speak? On whose behalf? I have escaped thus
far the ridicule of naming. I remain as your servant, your master, your —

LI

A Dove

In the first instance, a herald of free enterprise. Although barely perceptible, cracks soon appear. This is the nature of symbol. What is holiness in a city built of right angles? A monument to flesh. Zero enters as a cipher.

Second: in threadbare disguise, the principles of choice theory. Water enables a shift in foundation.

The third instance is a bastard, a composite. An early Picasso superimposed with a wire grid that is not a grid but a claw and it tightens around the throat of the Ideal. I am held inside a room of mirrors. What price a geometry of thought? What price these tongues of flame?

LII

The Severn

Although the city is built on sacred ground, initial evaluations are based on soil composition. Verdure. A pinwheel.

Design in medical robes walking the July highway. Canned goods wrapped in blue construction paper. Cinnamon. The bends. Correspondence on oak leaves unsent and crisp at the side of the bed. An expired insurance policy bound in twine at the dead letter office. Our shared ambulance. Their holiday in the sun.

Beretta, as Matisse, replacing typewriter keys to more readily express curvature. A school house in disrepair: we saw several rooms emptied of light and moisture.

The rivers survived due to their capacity for uncertainty. In Kentucky a train derails. These are feats of which science can give no account. The defence calls Dresden. These rituals we employ to carry our dead.

LIII

A Peacock

Flight as a weightless predicate. Is an arc by its nature complete? A relative of submersion from which to pursue the Ideal. When facing a mirror, the poem turning and dying.

The brute meeting of two distinct ideologies.
The colonial impulse of Design.
The insolvency of petroleum in water.
The bridges are closing above me.

We exist in abstraction but intersect the tangible in love, death and song.
Over Kentucky, a visible network of wires across the sky.
A persistence of yellow sepals.
The moment shall be decided but I cannot touch it.

I reach out, but I cannot touch it.

LIV

Celandine

There can be no resolution because there can be no because there can.
Once the origin grows fluid, any point fore or aft may be offered as
such. In its place, a standard repetition: Idolatry prompts Deuteronomy.
Deuteronomy prompts Migration. She has in time taken many names.
The greatest of these is —

A yellow cord through the foul canal.
There is another, now, at the window.

There are lilacs in the desert.
She will not turn away.

She will bring no resolution, only intersection.

Her song cannot end.
It is not begun.

ACKNOWLEDGEMENTS

Portions of this text were first published in *H_ngm_n*, *Word for Word*, *No Tell Motel*, *Re:Po*, *Past Simple*, *Bombay Gin*, and *Watching the Wheels: A Blackbird*. *The Margaret Thatcher Trilogy* was originally published as a limited edition chapbook by Catfish Press, August 2007. *The History of Zero* was originally published in an artist's edition limited to 75 copies by Candle-Aria Press, October 2008.

Thanks to Jim Goar and Leah Candelaria-Tyler for the original limited editions of these pieces. Thanks also to all who influenced or supported this writing through their various interactions with it, most notably Stacy Elaine Dacheux, H. Perry Horton, Jesse Morse, Eric Baus, Neelanjana Banerjee, Erik Anderson, Bhanu Kapil, Erik Noonan, Ryan Newton, Jackie Newton, Rohini Gupta, Christine Froude, David Froude, and Katie Froude. Also to Kathryn Mayo Winter and Doug Winter for the use of their art on the cover, and to Daniel, Rebsie and all at Skylight for seeing this book into print.

Richard Froude was born in London and raised in the West Country. He moved to the US in August 2002 at age 23. He lives in Denver, Colorado with his wife Rohini.

Also by Richard Froude:

Tarnished Mirrors: Translations of Charles Baudelaire
FABRIC: Preludes to the Last American Book